The Accomplished Muskrat Trapper

The Accomplished Muskrat Trapper

A Book on Trapping
for Amateurs

Arno E. Schmidt

with a foreword from
Kyle François

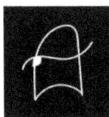

Long Day Press
Chicago

Published by Long Day Press
Chicago, Il 60647
LongDayPress.com
@LongDayPress

ISBN 978-1-950987-42-9 (Paperback Edition)
ISBN 979-8-8689-6103-8 (eBook Edition)

Cover and Layout by Joshua Bohnsack

Printed in the United States of America.
First Long Day Press Edition

PROUD MEMBER

[clmp]

CONTENTS

FOREWORD

> That is, I don't think I can learn from a
> wild animal how to live in particular—
> shall I suck warm blood, hold my tail
> high, walk with my footprint precisely
> over the prints of my hands?—but I
> might learn something of mindlessness,
> something of the purity of living in
> the physical senses and the dignity of
> living without bias or motive.
>
> — Annie Dillard
> from "Living like Weasels"[1]

In 1922 Arno Erdman Schmidt published *The Accomplished Muskrat Trapper*. The focus of this one-hundred and one year old text is only the muskrat. A small aquatic animal; I'm urging the reader not to blanch at the book's specificity. Truth in the specific. Consider Fernando Pessoa:

> There's infinity in a cell or a desert. one
> can sleep cosmically against a rock.[2]

[1] Annie Dillard, *Teaching a Stone to Talk*, 1982.
[2] Fernando Pessoa, *The Book of Disquiet*, 1982

I think that's right. There's an infinity in a muskrat and in the grading of raw fur. One can sleep cosmically within the pages of this book. Reading *The Accomplished Muskrat Trapper* properly — which is to say critically and with one's whole head — readers employ a similar skill-set as conscientious fur-harvesters: an organic interest and a serious attention to detail.

Growing up on the farm, a sixty-acre homestead in North-central Iowa, we maintained the timber and sandy farm ground with a certain honor, despite the inconsistent yields of the Wapsipinicon's flood plains. The pine trees and hardwoods, wildlife and foraging, contrasted distinctly from Mom and Dad's large Iowan families. My parents both grew up on farmland, surrounded by fields rather than woods. The woodland made our homestead different, and made Mom and Dad proud. We noted the types of birds, trees, edible (and inedible) fungi, the paths and trails of deer, raccoon, fox, coyotes, the channel geometry of the river, the patterns of seasonal flooding… during every season we were outside as much as possible, for essential and inessential reasons. First I learned to fish. How to tie a proper knot: what to keep, filet, and eat, what to unhook and release.

Carp were evasive and unless one had access to

a smoker (or was skilled in pickling) they were best left on the banks for the vultures, ospreys, and eagles. It was brutal to see the thin bones of a carp on the rocks, picked of its flesh, rotting out of its corpse, yet we understood the carp's relationship to the already precarious eco-system and the carp's propensity to out-compete every native species of aquatic life and destroy the river's diversity. Carp on the bank was a gesture to a healthy river — maybe pointless considering pollution and farm runoff — but still it was a gesture of ecological stewardship. Gardenism.

And, for us, trapping was the same thing. After two years on the farm, Dad found his old foothold traps. A trip to Grandma and Grandpa's brought back conifbears and a box trap. Meticulously we boiled, dyed, and waxed them. The process enlivened their previous functionality. We scouted the land before the trapping season started, looking for places we'd only catch what was intended to be caught. Dad taught us to read the land — how to visualize the animals moving — when we weren't there. We looked for signs delicately. It was important not to break branches or walk on trails. We looked for fresh paw prints. Raccoon scat told us what they ate and when. It's still a great pleasure knowing mink prints from muskrats' and raccoon prints from opossums'. I assume the general perception of the act is that it is brutal and primitive. But for us, for me, it was precise and subtle. A practical act in listening to and reading the land; a practical act of imagination. The best trappers I met were perceptive, quick-witted, and quiet.

In August of 2002, baseball season pushing toward playoffs yet before the leaves turned and fell, Dad took my brother Clint and me to a trapping seminar in Sigourney, Iowa. It was an all day educational session where we read informational pamphlets. I read about the animals in Iowa, their locations, habits, and populations. Over bland coffee and packaged mini-donuts, we learned about the ethical need for trappers; the practices and responsibilities these trappers embodied. I didn't have much of an opinion, but I remember a Xeroxed image of two barrels of apples. The left barrel was over-populated, rotting, spoiled. The second barrel was less populated, the apples could breathe, the fruit was hearty.

Of course the symbolism isn't too hard to put together. The barrels represented fur-bearing animals and their ecosystems. The over-populated barrel represented an environment ignored. The rotting apples were the undesirable deaths mammals suffered in the psueodomartial economy of Iowa's Big-AG: roadkill, rabies, and roundworm (to name a few that afflict rodents). The barrel metaphor is simplified and elementary. Even at twelve, I knew, the most unethical acts hide in the guise of ethical participation. The most damaging and vile poachers were people who *loved the land*. Later in the day we watched hands on demonstrations on how to catch them. I know there are obvious criticisms of the concept, yet I point to responsible stewardship of land and our ecosystems. Even if this stewardship is now a perverted retroactive attempt to manage failing systems of human invention.

A fleeting virtue; to strive for an acute understanding of our impact upon the world around us. I hope a skill-set is worth possessing during the production of natural goods, the process of artistic creation, forming communal bonds, when living. Arno Erdman Schmidt's book is a model of this skillset. His knowledge of the muskrat bleeds into infatuation. His skillset reflects his era, an era when fur harvesting was economically rewarding and also materially necessary.

A booklet that deals with raw materials and moves beyond the creek. He writes about the things forever at the center of all our passions and disciplines. *The Accomplished Muskrat Trapper* gifts diligent readers with a type of awareness that's all but absent in contemporary societies (severe, I know):

As we approach the familiar patch of

cat-tail flags, we hear the persistent crunch-crunch-crunch of tireless jaws, as they grind away at the juicy morsel of flag or water lily. We pause to listen, our little friend seems to be no more than twenty feet away. Further upstream we hear another and another in fact; the rushes seem to be alive with them...We stand motionless, as we discern a V-shaped streak of silvery lined ripples playing on the moonlit waters, heading directly toward us from the opposite shore. We know that the dark object at the head of this undulating formation is a muskrat, evidently bound on joining its friends at their feast in the rushes.[3]

The book balances practical advice for catching muskrats and clear-eyed depictions of their habitat. Schmidt's depictions exceed Thoreau's best descriptive passages. Perhaps because Thoreau had soft hands. *The Accomplished Muskrat Trapper* is written with an eye attuned to the material and economic realities of America. At his best Schmidt transcends any prescriptive lessons on how to catch muskrat; he

---

[3] A.E. Schmidt, *The Accomplished Muskrat Trapper*, 1922.

expresses a profound understanding of time, discipline, and patience. For Schmidt the muskrat swims directly toward massive profundities. A.E. Schmidt's study of the small rodent is a way to bear the ever-passing, grueling — forever grueling — nature of life on Earth. Like Charles Baudelaire says in *Be Drunk*[4]:

> You have to be always drunk. That's all there is to it—it's the only way. So as not to feel the horrible burden of time that breaks your back and bends you to the earth, you have to be continually drunk.
>
> But on what? Wine, poetry or virtue, as you wish. But be drunk.
>
> And if sometimes, on the steps of a palace or the green grass of a ditch, in the mournful solitude of your room, you wake again, drunkenness already diminishing or gone, ask the wind, the wave, the star, the bird, the clock, everything that is flying, everything that is groaning, everything that is rolling, everything that is singing, everything that is speaking... ask what

[4] Charles Baudelaire, "Enivrez-vous." *Le Spleen de Paris,* 1869.

> time it is and wind, wave, star, bird,
> clock will answer you: "It is time to be
> drunk! So as not to be the martyred
> slaves of time, be drunk, be continually
> drunk! On wine, on poetry or on virtue
> as you wish.

Most books aren't *great* (I know an ill-defined, perhaps worthless, measure to judge works of literature) and considering the hyper-evolving multitudes of knowledge bases, existing systems of production/consumption, and the saturation of systemic injustices (namely the failures of capitalism and the proliferation of systematic racism/bigotry/ fascism) few people publish *a* book and less publish a *great book*. Maybe *great book* is to say a book worth reading and rereading. These are books that do many things. They delight, but not simply, they inform, but not only, these are books not pinned down as a single thing, a *great book* changes as its reader changes, it's a special kind of mirror; it casts back the reader but is also a malleable fixture which shows itself *through* the reflection of the reader. A fixture that reflects and changes as many ways as there are readers, a humble reader is aware of their reflection through the mirror, or via the mirror, and how the mirror changes them.

These readers through the external, the physicality of language and of the book, are provided light. Great books are mirrors that radiate. I'm not being romantic.

I don't think A.E. Schmidt attempted to write this type of book. Arno would probably dismiss my previous analysis as over-scrutinized, or egg-headed, but he has no say now. We know even works conceived without lofty aspirations, a grandiose plan of greatness, still do important work. And keen, sensible, readers should consider two questions: Does your reading yield a harvest worth reaping? During your read does the muskrat move from the moonlit streams of the prairie and into the undefinable streams of your artistic imagination?

For a couple weeks I thought about these questions. It was late spring, the little booklet stayed on my person as a printed out manuscript. I worked the booklet like a trapline. I scouted it with a small ruler and various pencils. I marked the text in places that were lousy with my favorite passages, the profound ideas, and the practical advice. I recall now on a break from the bookstore; a grilled cheese, light beer, and maybe a bourbon; I had just found a moment in the text where I stopped and looked away. I was young again with Dad and Clint on the Wapsipinicon River. We were catching animals, or fishing, or chopping firewood, we were doing something in tow with how we intended it to go.

In pencil on the manuscript I marked the moments where I went back to a place really far away; I was thankful I could go there for a moment but didn't have to stay. It's these moments that allow me to say Arno Schmidt — very obviously — wrote a *great booklet* on how to catch muskrats.

Kyle François
Chicago
September 2023

INTRODUCTION

In placing this booklet before the great fraternity of American trappers, the author does not propose to exercise any pedagogical influence upon the truly professional trapper, who, seasoned in the hard school of experience, knows the animals he is seeking, like a mother knows her child. It is his wish, however, to assist and guide the amateur to a greater success.

Practically all text-books written for trappers, treating upon the subject of trapping and raw furs, heretofore have been neglectful of two things, namely, how to trap the animals under various conditions, and the assorting and grading of raw furs.

Of all fur bearers, the muskrat is the most numerous and least wary, hence very easily trapped — in consequence of this: it has been neglected by writers of trapping to a greater extent than any other fur-bearing animals. The author of *The Accomplished Muskrat Trapper* feels that he is instrumental in introducing to thousands of muskrat trappers a long-felt want. Being a trapper of wide experience, he early recognized the worth of the methods contained herein. Knowing that a fair trial will convince the most skeptical as to the merits and practicability of these methods, the writer feels sure that this little booklet will meet with the hearty approval of trappers everywhere.

Chapter 1.

Habits and Nature of the Muskrat.

The rodent quadruped muskrat, also known by the Indian name "Musquash" is a small amphibious animal of North America, being found as far north as Labrador and Alaska, and ranging south as far as the states of New Mexico and Arizona. There is only one species of the muskrat, but naturalists recognize several varieties or subdivisions, the differentia lying mainly in the color of the fur, firmness of the skin or pelt, and the physical dimensions of the animal. For example, the muskrats of the Atlantic coast states are comparatively large and of dark color; while those of the Northwest prairie region are smaller, thin and papery in pelt (except those living in clear or cold water streams) and of paler color. These variations are no doubt due to climatic and local conditions under which the animal lives.

Generally speaking, it may be said that the muskrat is a nocturnal animal, but where they are plentiful they are frequently observed prowling or swimming about during the day. It is found at home in rivers, lakes and ponds. When inhabiting the former it lives in burrows dug in the banks; the entrance to these are usually several feet under water. They are found to be most numerous in swamps which are heavily bordered with grasses and thickly strewn with scattering growths of aquatic vegetation. The roots of these plants compose the principal diet of the animal, while the tops furnish the material for the construction of their homes. The marsh 'rat differs in its mode of living from that of its brother the "river 'rat," by its habit of constructing dome-like houses. This change in abode is due to the natural environment in which it lives. In many large swamps scores of these queer little dwellings can be seen towering above the water. They average about three feet in height, and are composed of the roots and stems of grasses, reeds, wild rice and flags. The entrances are located under water. From four to eight 'rats are generally found in one house.

The muskrat is a herbivorous animal. Its food consists of the roots of flags, water lilies, etc. It is also very fond of sweet apples and vegetables, and will often raid a garden when located near its haunts. It is also partial to grain, especially corn.

Although the muskrat is herbaceous by nature, it is known to eat the flesh of clams. These it carries upon shore, deposits them in a pile in some secluded retreat and leaves them to die, whereupon they are easily opened and devoured with much avidity. The general assumption is that the animal eats these clams only when other food is scarce. This, however, is entirely in discord with the observations of the author, who has on several occasions discovered 'rats feeding on clams when their favorite food was plentiful. Therefore, it is only logical to presume, that it is not the lack of food that attracts the 'rat's attention to the lowly clam, but it is the abundance of the mussel in itself.

Muskrats are our most prolific fur bearers, producing from two to three litters in a season, the first making its appearance in the latter part of April or early May. The period of gestation requires about forty-five days. The young of the early spring litters will frequently rear one family during the same season. It is this progeny of these young females that accounts for the numerous kitts (immature muskrats) taken during the early part of the trapping season.

Considering the wonderful procreative powers of this little animal, it appears that they would become as numerous as the proverbial "hair on a dog's back," but they have many enemies, of which man with his traps and firearms is the most deadly, with perhaps the mink a close second. Many a time has the writer in his ramblings come onto a 'rat house, which had a small round boring at the water-line, just large enough to allow the long, slender body of a mink to pass through. To the casual observer this would appear to be merely a hole, but to the trained eye of the trapper it reveals a tale of woe. He knows that here, during the long, tranquil hours of the night, another family of muskrats was sacrificed to satisfy the flagrant craving of this bloodthirsty member of the weasel tribe. When a mink enters a house or burrow, in the aforesaid manner, the inhabitants flee by way of the diving hole. If everything remains quiet, they will return, one by one, to their home in a very few minutes. The crafty mink, knowing the nature of the muskrat, crouches near the diving hole, remaining very quiet, and bounces upon the poor, unsuspecting victims as they emerge.

Occasionally a trapper may come upon the remains of a muskrat and, following an investigation, cannot detect any clues as to the identity of the assailant. When there are no telltale tracks about, then it is safe to assume that the marauder was an owl or some other bird of prey.

The otter, fox and coyote can also be listed as enemies of the muskrat, as they too make an occasional capture.

With the above facts in mind, it can be easily understood that approximately only fifty per cent of all muskrats born ever reach maturity. In spite of all this, they manage to hold their own and are found in fair numbers in the rat producing sections.

The animal instincts of the muskrat are not as keenly developed as those of the designing fox or the wary mink. Unlike the beaver and otter, it is not afraid of civilization and thrives in the most thickly settled sections.

Nature in its entirety is wonderful. It is not unlike a vast panorama of charm and beauty. Here we find the ancient law — the survival of the fittest — a reality. Many people surmise the muskrat to be very uninteresting. But those people who are willing to devote a little of their time to the nocturnal study of the animal will surely acknowledge it to be a very interesting little creature. Where can we find the lover of nature whose heart would not be thrilled as we quietly make our way along some moonlit stream in the late fall (this being the time of year when 'rats are very busy) to get a glimpse at the home life of this little fur bearer? As we approach the familiar patch of cat-tail flags, we hear the persistent crunch-crunch-crunch of tireless little jaws, as they grind away at the juicy morsel of flag or water lily. We pause to listen, our little friend seems to be no more than twenty feet away. Further upstream we hear another and another in fact; the rushes seem to be alive with them. Some of them are cutting down the stems of wild rice and flags, while others are dragging the material away to build and repair their houses with it. We stand motionless, as we discern a V-shaped streak of silvery lined ripples playing on the moonlit waters, heading directly toward us from the opposite shore. We know that the dark object at the head of this undulating formation is a muskrat, evidently bound on joining its friends at their feast in the rushes. Hark! There is a sudden commotion in the flags, followed by a splash and a plunge; then all is still, the grinding has ceased, the silvery ripples have faded away and the water is smooth and reflectent, not unlike a great mirror. We are surprised and wonder at the cause of the sudden alarm, which drove the 'rats to the sheltering depths of the river. Had we not remained perfectly quiet? We turn, just in time to see a monstrous owl glide noiselessly by the moon.

running

walking

Fig. 1

Chapter 2.

Trapping Muskrats

Open Water Methods.

There are numerous methods employed in trapping the muskrat; most of them will prove successful when they are used under the proper conditions, time and place. The muskrat being a member of the amphibious class of animals, consequently traps must be set in or very near the water to attain the best results. This, however, does not mean that traps set at random will bring results, but, on the other hand, when sets are properly placed at signs, then the novice can rest assured that he will be rewarded for his efforts.

When a trapper decides to operate on a certain stretch of water, his first duty would be to study the signs of the animal, from the abundance or scarcity of which he can closely estimate the number of animals present in that particular locality, also the size of territory he can handle, and the number of traps required to cover the same.

What are signs? They are the visible indications which betray the presence of the animals, such as tracks in the muddy margins of the shore (see Fig. 1), feed beds, houses, dens, slides, the freshly cut stems of aquatic vegetation and excremental matter on logs, drift wood, rocks, and other objects lying in or near the water. To become expert at reading signs requires practical experience; theory or book knowledge alone will not do. The success or failure of any trapper can be measured by his ability to read the signs of the animals he is seeking and his knowledge of their nature.

Our next consideration will be the selection of the proper traps. When trapping muskrats with the common steel traps, never use anything larger than size No. 1 1/2 nor smaller than size No. 1.

The "Newhouse" is without a doubt the best and most reliable all around steel trap on the market; the material and workmanship embodied in its construction, combined with its durability, render it a product of the highest character.

The "Victor" is the most popular of the cheaper kind of traps and is generally used by those who follow trapping as a side-line. While trapping 'rats, many trappers prefer the Victor to the Newhouse, on account of the latter's powerful spring. The forelegs of the muskrat are comparatively small and frail and easily broken off; for that reason too strong a spring is not desired.

The various makes of "jump" traps are rapidly becoming very popular. They are a very compact trap on account of their feature of having the spring on the inside of the jaws, which permits them to be set in places where other traps could only be set with great difficulty.

There are many brands of traps manufactured which possess special features, such as double jaws, webbed jaws, high grip, etc. All of these traps are excellent for catching muskrats, as they are made to prevent the animals from gnawing or wringing off, and thus escaping.

One of the best traps for muskrats ever invented is manufactured by W. A. Gibbs & Son, Chester, Penn. It is made with two sets of jaws; the inner set gripping the animal's leg, while the outer set clutches the body. From this trap there is no escape when once caught, in many cases killing its victim instantly, which benevolent feature makes it a favorite of many.

Trapping methods may be classified into two separate groups, namely, blind and bait sets, ranking in the order named. A blind set is arranged at signs without the use of bait. Traps placed in position so as to guard the approach to food and scent decoys are termed bait sets.

Scent decoys, better known as animal baits, are compounded of various ingredients which appeal to the inborn and irresistible instincts of the animals, and which assist in enticing them to traps.

The following methods are recognized to be the best and most reliable for trapping 'rats when streams are free of ice. They will prove their merits to the beginner when applied intelligently. While the muskrat is generally conceded to be one of the easiest of fur bearers to trap, let no one suppose that the careless trapper who makes his sets in a sort of hit or miss fashion, will ever achieve much of a success in trapping them.

Perhaps the most common method employed in the capture of this little animal, is to set traps at the foot of their slides, in two or three inches of water. A slide, in the trapper's vocabulary, is a place on the banks frequented by 'rats, usually extending from eight to sixteen inches above the water and having a kind of plastic perch or rest at the top, upon which are generally found excrements of the animal. These slides are easily recognized on account of their worn and smooth appearance, which is brought about by the animal's habit of sliding into the water when leaving them. Do not waste any time in setting traps at old and dried signs, those that are being used will appear damp and often sprinkled with fresh mud. Where the water is not deep enough at the foot of the slide to completely cover the trap, excavate a bed for the same to the desired depth. This rule should be followed in all forms of water sets. Whenever possible, always stake the trap chain into deep water at full length, as the first impulse of the captured game is to seek shelter by diving into deep water, where, following a short struggle, the weight of the trap finally drowns it. The sliding pole is another and more certain method of drowning the animals (See Fig. 2). Drowning will not only conceal the captured game from possible thieves, but also secure it for the trapper against gnawing and wringing off, and last, but not least, this humane act will do away with a lot of needless suffering.

Fig. 2

Another good way to take them is at their feed beds. These are located near shore among the scattering growths of aquatic vegetation. They appear to be floating in the water semi-submerged, and are composed of the refuse of the animal's food, such as the stems of blue flags, wild rice, reeds and bits of various grasses found growing near their haunts. When making sets on these beds make sure that the traps are from one to two inches under water, as this will allow the trap to get a higher grip on the animal's outstretched leg. Arrange the set so that the catch will drown.

Often while looking for signs the trapper will come upon a small, narrow path, which is three to five inches in width, leading from the water to some other body of water near by, or taking its course across a peninsula to again terminate in the water on the other side. Such a trail is commonly made and used by muskrats. When you find such a place, set a trap in the water at each end of the trail. When making a set where the water is much deeper than the usual depth required, take sticks about twelve inches long and twice the caliber of an ordinary lead pencil, shove these into the bank horizontally about a third of their length and three inches under water, placing them an inch apart, six in a row. This will make a platform for the trap, which will overcome the danger of the animals passing over the set without getting caught.

In the late fall when 'rats are busy building and repairing their houses, they can be caught by setting the trap on that side of the structure showing the greatest slope; because here they ascend when at their labor. When staking the trap at a set of this nature, it is advisable to drive another stake about a foot beyond the first. The animal, when caught, struggling winds the chain around the outer stake, and is thus hindered from reaching the house, where it otherwise would do great damage, tearing and digging into it. This would result in frightening the other inmates away, thus lessening the trapper's chances of duplicating his catch.

The washes under banks and the undermined roots of trees at the water's edge, created by the ceaseless toil of the elements, afford good places to set traps, as every passing 'rat will visit such places. Traps should be set and covered very carefully, as a place of this nature is often investigated by the elusive mink and inquisitive raccoon. As a consequence, the trapper has a fine opportunity of catching a more valuable animal.

When searching the stream for signs, you will often notice the droppings of the animals on logs and scraps of lumber lying in the water. These can be converted into excellent sets by cutting a bed for the trap with the ax, just far enough under water to completely cover the trap.

When signs and places as described above are scarce, but muskrats are known to exist, proceed as follows: At some conspicuous place, dig a horizontal hole in the bank right at the water-line, which should be about a foot deep and five inches in diameter. Pin a piece of parsnip, carrot, cabbage or sweet apple, back in the hole. Some trappers use a piece of the flesh of muskrat, the scent of which is attractive to muskrats. Set the trap at the mouth of this hole, in two or three inches of water, conceal carefully by covering lightly with water-soaked leaves and thin mud. The above is a set equally good for mink, as this animal has the habit of exploring every hole that it comes to in its travels.

Another and most simple method, is merely to fasten the bait on the bank about eight inches above the trap. In reaching for the bait the 'rat will step into the trap and get caught.

Some trappers prefer to use animal baits in connection with their 'rat sets at all times. This, I believe, is wholly unnecessary, excepting during mating, which occurs the latter part of February and extends throughout the rest of the trapping season. At this time, a good, dependable scent will help considerably in luring animals to traps.

There are numerous brands of scents on the market, some of which are reliable, but most of them are a farce, and are merely intended to pry hard-earned dollars from overalls pockets. The formula used in the manufacture of most of these baits is kept a secret by the makers. The purchaser, not knowing what ingredients they contain, faces the perplexing problem of choosing, or more frankly stated, guessing, as to their merits, when buying.

But, why worry about buying decoys when you can easily make them yourself? The musk of the muskrat is the best scent known for attracting this animal. It is found on both sexes, in two cream colored glands known as castors, which are located just under the skin of the belly. Remove these from every animal you catch, and place in an air-tight bottle or jar until needed. When you are ready to prepare the scent, proceed as follows: Mash the castors into a fine pulpy state; to every ounce of this mixture add two ounces of glycerine to give volume and prevent evaporation, also one grain of corrosive sublimate. Let stand for about a week and you will have the best muskrat scent obtainable. Cork tightly and keep in a cool place. Sprinkle a few drops of this scent at every set during the spring season.

In the early spring, as soon as the first heavy thaws

set in releasing the muskrats from their natural prison, they are eagerly sought because their pelts are at their best, being fully prime at this time of year. But trappers are often hampered in their operations against the lowly 'rat at this particular time, on account of the absence of signs. This drawback can be overcome as follows: Procure pieces of two by six (plank), each about four feet in length. Set two traps on each plank, one near each end, covering them lightly with dry grass or leaves. Sprinkle a few drops of scent along the plank between traps. Staple the traps to the ends of the plank and anchor the same near shore. Some trappers scatter pieces of bait on the plank, but this is not necessary, as the scent will draw them much better than food bait at this time of year.

Another method is to build a small mound in about six inches of water. This can be made of small stones, plastered with mud, and should extend about six inches above the water. Sprinkle a few drops of scent on top of mound and set trap at the bottom, staking into deep water.

Chapter 3.

Trapping Muskrats Under Ice in Winter.

The hustling trapper generally gathers a fair sized collection of muskrat pelts in the late fall, as 'rats are very active and move about a great deal at this time of the year, leaving signs in abundance at which the trapper may set his traps. Then suddenly some frosty morning as he makes his rounds, he finds the stream covered with a thin coat of ice, a sign heralding the arrival of winter. Under the thin ice the traps are setting and undisturbed just as he left them the day before. Disgusted he lifts them and quits. Right here is where many 'rat trappers make a mistake: When they find streams covered with ice, they pull stakes and quit. If these same trappers knew how to catch them under the ice, they could greatly increase their annual catch.

What becomes of the muskrat when its natural highway is covered with ice? How does it obtain its food while thus imprisoned? How can it breathe under water? Queries such as these are often put to trappers by those who are unacquainted with the nature of the animal. When streams are frozen, muskrats are practically shut off from the outside world, but nevertheless they are as happy as ever, playing and frolicking in the water and often traveling great distances from their burrows. When hungry they seek the beds of wild rice and flags, from which they procure their food. This they carry to their feed beds or dens to be devoured. They cannot breathe in the water as fish do, because they are not endowed with gills, but they do travel long distances under the same breath, and when the lungs have drained the oxygen, the 'rat comes up to the under side of the ice and exhales. The bubble thus formed immediately fills with oxygen and is then again inhaled, whereupon the animal continues on its journey until it finds it necessary to repeat the operation.

As soon as the ice is sufficiently strong enough to bear a man's weight, many muskrats are taken by men and boys who get out on the ice armed with clubs and pursue the animals as they swim along under the ice; when a 'rat comes up to the ice to replenish its supply of oxygen, a sharp blow from a well-seasoned club brought down on the ice directly above the animal will stupefy it. While the animal is in this temporary state of coma, a hole is cut in the ice and the victim taken out. When hunting 'rats in this manner, I prefer to use a shotgun in place of the club, because it is quicker in action and the terrific concussion which occurs when the shot strikes the ice often kills the game outright. As many as a dozen 'rats are often taken by one man in the course of a few hours, as they seem to move about more freely during the day, when streams are covered with ice. In their eagerness to get their share of the pelts, trappers often receive a wetting while pursuing the animals over thin ice. When operating on thin ice stay in the shallow places; remember the watchword "safety first."

Sometimes muskrats are driven from their dens by pounding the bank with some heavy object directly over the entrance; when the animals are aware of the thumping, they usually flee from imaginary harm's way by taking to the water; they are then shot as they emerge. The above methods of taking muskrats through ice are good, but can only be used on clear ice, not over five inches in thickness, as the shot will not take effect in heavier ice.

While open water trapping cannot be excelled, in comparison to results obtained, under-ice trapping will adequately repay those who are willing to give it a fair trial. No trapper should attempt to make sets under ice which is much more than a foot in thickness, as the task would prove too elaborate. The following methods will bring results when instructions are followed carefully. They are being used by expert trappers and are the only practical modes for this sort of trapping:

Setting traps at the mouth of dens is perhaps the best and most profitable under-ice method known to the trapping fraternity, as it will be remembered that the average den contains from four to eight muskrats, and in some instances even more. Therefore it can be readily understood that the trapper who will locate dens in his spare time during the summer and fall will be the most successful. While hunting dens in open water use either a boat or hip boots; select a quiet day when the water is calm, travel slowly along near shore, keeping watch for the mouth of dens. These entrances are usually from one to four feet under water. If the den is inhabited, the entrance will be found clear of all rubbish and obstructions of any kind. Many of these holes have a trench-like trail or run extending a yard or two towards midstream. Whenever a den is found, mark the same by shoving a stick on the upstream side of the entrance, the top of which should extend about ten inches above the water level to allow for a sudden rise of the stream. When dens are thus marked they can be easily found after ice forms.

Many dens can also be found through clear ice, as follows: Walk along on the ice near shore until you see a streak of bubbles under the ice, which is several yards in length, usually extending towards midstream; further examination will reveal the mouth of den at the termination of the bubble stream near the shore. Mark dens with stakes as described above. The traps are lowered into the mouth of den at the end of a four-foot piece of wire, said end being shaped into a hook for holding the trap; or, better still, purchase a "Triumph Trap Placer," which is manufactured by the Triumph Trap Co., of Oneida, New York. This is a very handy instrument, used for the setting of traps in difficult places, especially under ice. In all den sets, the trap should be placed inside the entrance as far as it is possible to get it. A wide entrance often allows the game to pass over the trap without getting caught. This can be overcome by placing flat stones under the traps or by obstructing the upper half of the entrance with a wide trap stake, which is pushed into the side of entrance in a horizontal manner. This compels the game to dive under it and pass low enough to get caught. The traps are fastened by slipping the chain ring on to the stake which marks the den.

When the ice is covered with snow, dens cannot be located as described above. In that case a fair number of dens can often be found by sounding. This is accomplished by pounding the ice with the

52

ax in shallow places along the shore, until you find a place which produces a hollow sound upon being struck; this indicates a 'rat run. When you find such a place, cut through and set a trap in the run, then cover the hole in the ice, using sticks and dry grass as a foundation and then pack tightly with snow. A run is the trench-like trail under water which leads to the mouth of den. When these runs are located in shallow water, the body heat of the animals melts the ice to the extent of several inches directly above the run. This creates an air space which accounts for the hollow sound when struck from above.

The barrier set will capture both the muskrat and mink, traveling under the ice. Every experienced trapper knows that these animals swim along near shore in their travels, for various reasons, chiefly while hunting for food. The set is as follows: Cut a narrow channel in the ice about six feet in length; begin at the bank and work out towards midstream. Now take sticks and build a barrier the entire length of channel, shove them down well into the bottom about an inch apart, leaving the tops an inch or two above the level of the ice. Leave an opening about six inches wide, twelve or eighteen inches from the bank, in about six inches of water. In this opening set your trap. An animal coming along will find this opening, attempt to pass through and get caught. This set will bring the best results when used on small streams and drainage canals, as these can be staked their entire width. When staking small streams, leave an opening for a trap on each side of the stream. Fasten traps by slipping the chain ring into the stake at opening. When the water where the set is to be made is somewhat deeper than eight inches, place flat stones or similar objects under traps. This should be done to crowd the animals into the traps. When the ice gets heavier, thus lessening the water space, then these obstacles must be removed. Cover the holes in the ice as stated above. It is advisable, also much easier, to construct the barriers shortly before the streams freeze up.

On warm winter days muskrats often come forth to sun themselves; they remain but a few moments at a time, but that is sufficient to catch them in traps which are properly placed in the water at springs, air holes and rapids, also at the inlets and outlets of lakes and ponds.

In many lakes and swamps muskrats live in houses instead of burrows. To trap them in their houses, cut a hole on the south side of the house, then set the trap inside on the bed or in the diving hole. Fasten the trap to a clog on the outside of the house, then tightly close the opening with the material cut away;

on top of this freely pack dry grass or reeds and then snow. This must be done to keep the diving hole from freezing. The traps should be visited at least twice a day, preferably in the morning and in the evening, because the animals do not always drown when caught in this way. Before you decide to set traps in houses, better look up the statute of your state in regard to this matter. Many states have now enacted a law making it unlawful for any person, at any time, to destroy, molest or set traps in or upon muskrat houses.

Where muskrats are plentiful, they are often taken by lowering the traps through the ice, in three or four feet of water. These traps are baited with a piece of carrot or cabbage, which is bound to the pedal of the traps. The muskrats prowling along the bottom of the stream investigate the dainty morsel and are caught. The best traps to use for this method are the "Two Triggers" and "Alligator" game traps, because these traps clutch the animal's body. Should you use the common steel trap, be sure you use nothing small than size No. 1 1/2, because the game is usually caught by the head. The trigger of the trap should be set very lightly, so it will spring at the slightest pressure. This method is most generally used near muskrat houses, in states where the law prohibits the setting of traps in these houses.

Chapter 4.

Opportunity
and
'Rat Ranching.

The annual catch of North American raw furs has a monetary value of approximately twenty-five million dollars. The number of pelts required to reach such a figure must necessarily be very large. Trapping is done, more or less, by many people, in many walks of life, who follow the sport for both profit and pleasure; from the professional pelt hunter, down to the farmer's boy, who during the winter indulges in trapping as a side line, tending his traps between chores.

The fur business is and always has been an important cog in American industry. It furnishes employment for thousands, from the trapper to the buyer, manufacturer and retailer; but there is now a cloud of depression threatening on the horizon of the industry. Fur-bearing animals, which at one time roamed our prairies, streams and woodlands, in seemingly unlimited numbers, are now rapidly becoming very scarce, where a few years previous they were very plentiful. The beaver and several other species of fur bearers are already threatened with extinction and are doomed to follow in the wake of the passenger pigeon and bison, unless something extremely radical is done in the way of game preservation in comparison to present-day methods. What has brought about this rapid diminution in the ranks of fur-bearing animals? It is the rapid advance of civilization which deprives the fur bearers of their natural haunts. It is the inventive genius of Americans, who, with highly efficient traps, guns, especially prepared poisons, smoke-torpedoes and other ingenious devices, contribute to deplete the ranks of the animals; the numerous fur houses throughout the country, flooding the mails with their propaganda urging everyone to trap. We can hardly scan the columns of a paper or magazine during the fur months but what our gaze will fall upon an alluring display of raw fur advertisements. These announcements are continually calling for unlimited quantities of raw furs; they are ever urging men and boys to push their trapping operations to the utmost. These concerns are giving free advice to beginners; they offer free instructions in the art of trapping the fur bearers. All this has had but one result: The fabulous prices paid for raw furs and the extensive advertising in recent years have kindled a crusade on our fur bearers which has developed a crisis. When trapping is carried on to the extreme folly of taking the animals which should be left for breeding, then our natural supply of "wild fur" shall cease to be perpetual.

And that is just what is taking place, in spite of the legislation passed in favor of the fur bearers — in spite of the laws which have been enacted for their protection by the various states and territories. In the light of this fact, the question arises: Where are the millions of pelts to come from that the world needs each year? The time is not far off when the demand will exceed the supply. How can we keep an industry alive that can use millions of dollars' worth of raw furs annually, thus furnishing employment for thousands of people? There is only one remedy, and that is — fur farming.

Fur farming is by no means a new idea. Farsighted men experimented with fur bearers early in the seventies. Many people advance the theory that the animals will not breed or thrive in captivity; but this argument is not sound; we need only remember that all our domestic animals were wild creatures at one time.

True, fur farming, like any other business, has its drawbacks; but these impediments are rapidly conquered by the persistent and energetic study and scientific research of enthusiastic men, who are devotedly interested in the welfare of the animals, and the evolution of the industry to a higher and better standard. In any case, the injury is not beyond the remedy. For example, some of the early pioneers in the business felt very much dejected when they discovered that the animals did not fur properly in captivity. This was later found to be due to crowded and improper quarters, improper drainage and the lack of shade about the enclosures. This has been remedied to the extent that ranch raised fur now excels the "wild" in quality and beauty. This testimony is verified by the fact that the sum of $3,800 was paid for the pelt of a single "ranch bred" silver fox; a sum that has never been realized for the pelt of a wild fox of like variety.

Cannibalism among the animals was another evil fur farmers had to contend with. This was traced to be due to the feeding of improper foods, and especially underfeeding.

Abortion must also be guarded against. During pregnancy strangers must be kept away from the ranch, because during this period females become very suspicious of them and are nervous and restless, often injuring themselves when thus excited. This trouble is most common among animals which were procured in the wilds. Each succeeding generation of ranch raised stock becomes more and more domesticated; consequently the keeper finds it much easier to win their confidence.

Practically all the failures in fur farming are due to the lack of experience of the people thus engaged; their failure to take the proper interest in the animals, so they may understand them and their requirements.

There are now numerous fur farms located throughout the northern part of the United States and Canada. These establishments propagate and improve the breed of fox, skunk, muskrat, raccoon, mink and opossum.

Fox ranching is the leading branch of this industry. There are many ranches which specialize in high grade foxes, such as black, silver, cross and red. Prince Edward Island is the center of this industry; the most valuable foxes in the world are ranched here, being the result of careful and selective breeding. John A. Lea, of Summerside, P. E. Island, is recognized as one of America's leading authorities on the question. He is a man of wide experience and knows the animals like a mother knows her flock. In his "Facts About Foxes" Mr. Lea says:

(A) "Fox ranching is an industry begun in P. E. Island in the 80's.

(B) "Raising domesticated silver foxes is now an established success.

(c) "Since 1909 millions of dollars have been paid in fox dividends.

(d) "The domesticated silver fox is tame and easily cared for.

(e) "Foxes will eat anything the ordinary dog will eat.

(f) "The average litter is from three to four pups.

(g) "The total annual increase is about 100 per cent.

(h) "It is possible to breed up or improve any kind of foxes.

(i) "The foxes now ranched on P. E. Island are valued at $6,000,000.

(j) "These foxes earned $2,500,000 for their owners in 1920.

(k) "The average profit to the fox rancher is about 40 per cent annually."

The above facts show that fox ranching is not a dream, but an established success, paying large dividends on the capital invested. This is also true about fur farming in general. There are many cases on record showing the wonderful results obtained by men who experimented with skunk, mink and muskrats.

Especially is this true of the muskrat. I shall endeavor to set forth here the possibilities 'rat ranching offers to those of small means. In the large salt water marshes along the Atlantic coast and Chesapeake Bay, 'rat ranching has been carried on systematically for many years. This marsh land which was at one time considered practically valueless is now yielding large returns annually. The animals are protected from possible poachers by the authorities and land owners. They are trapped only when the fur is at its best. The owners see to it that enough animals are left for breeding. Wicomico, Dorchester, and Sommersett Counties (Maryland) compose the center of this industry. The value of the catch in any one of these counties runs Into thousands of dollars yearly. And It must be remembered that this is from land which at one time sold from state or government at thirty cents an acre.

The following are extracts from a letter by a well known manufacturer of game traps, who owns a large muskrat preserve In Maryland. I shall put down these statements, not to encourage anyone to go there, as the ground is well occupied and trappers are numerous, but merely to serve as an illustration of what can be done with the numerous swamps, ponds and small lakes scattered throughout the rest of the United States and Canada, and which are now considered practically worthless:

> "Good muskrat marsh in Maryland, where the writer's place is located. Is selling now for from twenty to thirty dollars an acre... As a general proposition the owners lease their marshes to the trappers for a certain part of the catch, which has up to the present time been anywhere from one-half to two-thirds to the owners... The marshes never dry up, because they are only a very few feet above sea level and a great many of them are overflowed at times by extremely high tides... My 'rats are in an open marsh and I do not furnish them any feed, or look after them in any way, except to try to keep the dogs and foxes out of It and to catch the hawks, owls and eagles that prey on them. The marsh furnishes plenty of natural feed, and the only thing that is necessary to do is simply to keep their enemies away and they take very good care of themselves... There are a great many natural marshes along the east coast of the country, in New Jersey, Delaware,

Maryland and Virginia especially, these marshes have been inhabited by muskrats probably since their creation."

Now then, from the above statements we can readily conceive that the raising of muskrats is the simplest form of fur farming, requiring very little capital to get started. For these reasons: First, it does not necessitate the construction of expensive pens and enclosures; second, animals need not be fed — the food supply is natural; third, a keeper is not required — the animals take care of themselves.

As prospective 'rat ranchers, our first duty would be the selection of the proper site for the ranch. This would naturally be in the form of a lake, marsh or pond. Many farmers have such a body of water on their land; these vary in size from a few acres to several hundred. Those who contemplate raising 'rats, but do not own a proper site, could easily buy one at a reasonable figure, as most people consider such property of little value. Before buying a pond or marsh which you are not familiar with, investigate whether it has any inlets, such as springs and small streams. A marsh or small lake which is likely to dry up during a drought is not to be considered, as the 'rats would then be forced to leave it. Some of these waters have no visible means of support, yet they hold the same level of water year after year. This seems to be due to the nature of their location or else they are fed by inner springs. When in doubt about a certain marsh or lake, better talk with several neighbors who are familiar with it, before buying; they may, from observation, be able to give you reliable information about the water supply.

Many lakes and ponds which are possessed of an inlet and outlet are often burdened with a very high level of water, and then again at other times not enough. This water could be held to a normal level by putting a dam across the outlet. This dam, however, would need protection against the burrowing mania of the muskrats, as they would soon have it looking like a sponge; the only difference would be, that the sponge holds water, while the dam would not. Such a dam could be amply protected with a solid covering of rocks. These should average in size anywhere from a baseball to a man's head, and should cover the dam to a depth of about two feet. This layer of rocks should also extend along the bottom of the stream on both sides of the dam to a distance of about twenty feet. The building of such a structure would require some hard labor and time, but would well pay for itself where the ranch in question is large enough to warrant its construction.

Following the selection of the proper site, our next consideration would be the food supply. Most lakes, marshes and ponds are naturally conducive to wild rice, flag and water lily growth. These aquatic plants are the mainstay of the muskrat's food supply; they also represent the material of which they construct their houses.

Should the prospective 'rat ranch be devoid of such vegetation, as is sometimes the case, the owner should at once take steps to encourage its growth by Introducing some flags and water lilies. These should be planted in about one foot of water and one yard apart. It is advisable to plant them along the shore, in several patches of two or three rows each, and numbering about fifty plants to the patch. These plants, when once started, will multiply very rapidly and spread into deeper water. The best time to do this work of transplanting is in the spring, just before the plants start sprouting. During the summer green grass is eaten by muskrats with great relish; therefore, mixed grass seed should be sown liberally wherever the banks are barren. The seed of wild rice should also be sown in the fall of the year, shortly after it is gathered. Wild rice will grow in deeper water than flags, and all that is necessary to start it is to scatter the seed in a depth of several feet of water. It is good policy to sow some wild rice every fall, even when the supply of food is ample, as 'rats are very fond of the myriads of young tender sprouts which shoot up in the spring. In waters where the food supply must be developed, it is advisable to keep muskrats away for at least one year, because their presence would greatly hamper its progress.

When the food supply has been well established, we are ready to stock up our ranch. The 'rats can be purchased or procured by trapping. As a general rule, 'rats will already be found at home in a prospective ranch, which boasts of plenty of water and food; they find such a place by force of instinct, though the nearest stream may be fifty miles away.

We need pay no further attention to them, except to destroy their enemies, which in this case are, chiefly, the birds of prey. Sometimes these pirates of the air will establish headquarters at some muskrat marsh, and remain for weeks at a time. Selecting some lofty perch from which they can scan every angle of their acquired domain, they will often remain perfectly motionless, for hours at a time, only to hurl themselves upon the unwary muskrat as it makes its appearance on the water.

These intruders must be caught — but how? Occasionally we may be able to "check" up on one of them, with our old scattergun; but this is the exception to the rule, as these birds are far too wary to be approached in the open. Therefore we must resort to steel traps for their destruction. This is not as difficult as it would seem at first thought. Knowing their habit of alighting on the highest point of vantage while awaiting their prey, we proceed to set up poles in our marsh, which are about eight inches in diameter at the top. On the tops of these poles we conceal our traps (preferably jump traps), by covering them with water-soaked chaff or leaves. Pegs are driven into the sides of the poles, upon which we ascend when tending the traps. These poles need not be very high when they are set up in the open; eight or ten feet above the water would be sufficient, when there are no higher objects near. The erection of one such pole would suffice for every ten acres of territory.

The animals must also be protected against poaching and free trapping. It is a good idea to post signs of warning against trespassing on the premises. There should not be much trouble on this point, however, because people, as a whole, respect the property and rights of their fellow men.

When the animals are thus protected, they will increase very rapidly. A marsh or pond which is covered with a mixed growth of aquatic vegetation will naturally support a greater number of muskrats than a deep water lake where such vegetation can only be found along the shores.

Good marsh land has been known to produce an average of one hundred 'rats per acre annually, and in some instances even more, but such a yield is above the ordinary. Statistics show the average yield of 'rat pelts to be about fifteen per acre yearly. This number of animals can be safely trapped without fear of encroaching upon the necessary quota of animals required as breeders. Of course there are some waters that produce a much larger yield per acre, and these must be trapped accordingly. In a marsh or lake of low banks the 'rats are compelled to build houses. The owners of such a ranch can closely estimate the number of animals present by counting the houses and then multiplying the result by four.

Though the muskrat will tolerate more crowding than other fur-bearing animals, the owner should prevent overcrowding, otherwise some of them would leave for parts less crowded. Some raisers, while gathering their annual crop of fur, make it a point to trap only two-thirds of their grounds, and when this is exhausted of muskrats they quit. This method assures the owner sufficient breeding stock for the next crop, and at the same time prevents crowding the animals.

'Rat ranching is a business which does not require much money or effort to build up, and when once established there is very little to do, except to trap the muskrats during the proper season. The best time, in fact the most profitable time to do this, is in the early spring, when pelts are strictly prime and the fur is at its best.

Judging from the ever-increasing popularity of muskrat fur and the consequent rise in value, "rat ranching" can certainly be considered a profitable undertaking. Let us, for example, take into consideration a fifty-acre marsh, producing the low average of fifteen 'rats per acre. This would represent an annual crop of about seven hundred and fifty pelts. To trap this number of animals would require about thirty days. For eleven months out of the year, the owner would be free to take up any line of endeavor he may choose to follow. Considering the small amount of capital and time required for the establishment and upkeep of such a "vivarium," is there any other form of farming or stock raising more profitable? We venture the answer without fear of contradiction — there is absolutely not.

Chapter 5.

Handling
and Grading
Muskrat Fur.

Thousands of dollars are annually lost to trappers on account of the improper handling of raw fur. This is due to both ignorance and carelessness on the part of a certain class of trappers. If these amateurs would pay a little more attention to the proper way of killing and skinning the animals, and the proper fleshing, stretching and drying of the skins, they would realize from 5 to 10 per cent more on their furs.

When animals are found alive in traps they may be dispatched by a few sharp blows on the head with a stick, which should be smooth and free from knots and stubs, otherwise the fur is liable to be damaged. An animal when caught will often retreat under the banks or between root snags, and then there is always danger of the catch escaping by its violent struggles when the trapper attempts to dislodge it from its retreat. A .22 caliber pistol will prove very handy for just such emergencies; a bullet between the eyes from such a weapon will subdue the animal, whereupon it can be safely hauled out. There is no danger of decreasing the value of the fur when using such a small firearm.

Trapped muskrats are sometimes attacked, killed and torn to shreds by mink or owl, as these nocturnal prowlers are very fond of the flesh of these animals. When traps are not promptly looked after early in the day, magpies and crows will often stage a mass attack and peck and harass the poor victims to death. Such catches are a total loss to the trapper, who is in most part to blame, because of his carelessness in attending traps and his failure to arrange the sets so the entrapped animals may drown and be thus concealed from view.

Before skinning an animal, examine the carcass and make sure that the fur is clean and free from foreign matter. When an animal is bespattered with dried mud, proceed to remove the same by thoroughly brushing the fur; fresh mud and blood stains can be removed by rubbing and rinsing the carcass in cold water. Burs and other foreign matter should also be combed and brushed out. When this has been accomplished, we are ready to skin the animal.

There are two methods employed in skinning the various fur-bearers, namely, "open" and "cased." The former method is used on the larger animals, such as bear, wolverine, mountain lion, etc. The latter method is used on the smaller animals, which include our friend the muskrat. The blade of the skinning knife should possess a very keen edge at all times, so that there will be no ragged edges on the pelts. It is much easier and more agreeable to skin an animal right after it is killed, while the body heat is still retained. Never allow an animal to lay unskinned for more than twenty-four hours, as it is liable to taint, which has a tendency to cause the fur to slip. Such pelts would have little or no value

To skin the muskrat, cut the skin loose around the hind legs near the feet where the fur ends, then rip down the back of the hind legs to the root of the tail and loosen the fur around the same. Do not skin the tail of the muskrat, as this has no fur value. Now lay the knife aside and peel the skin with your fingers by drawing it down towards the head. You will find that it will peel very readily, with a little flesh here and there threatening to adhere to the skin; most of this can be held back by pushing the fingers of one hand against it, while pulling the skin with the other. To loosen the skin at the front legs, work the thumb of your right hand between the skin and the flesh on the underside of the main joint of the leg, and pull; the skin will come off very easily. The knife comes into play again when the ears are reached. These must be cut off at the base, close to the head. When cutting the skin loose around the eyes, care must be exercised to avoid dilating the apertures. Now peel down to the nose and jaws, and with the knife assist in peeling the skin from these members. The job of skinning is now complete and we have what is termed a cased pelt with the fur side in.

It is a deplorable fact that a large percentage of trappers do not use the knife when removing the skin from the head of the muskrat. They simply pull it off by sheer force, with the result that the skin generally tears off right back of the ears, which leaves a badly damaged pelt. Such pelts when marketed are thrown into the lower grades and sell for about 40 per cent less.

When the pelt is ready for fleshing, it is placed on the fleshing board. This board should be made of one-half-inch material about thirty inches long, four and one-half inches wide at the base and three and one-half inches wide at the shoulders. The upper end of the board should taper to a rounded point. The edges should be rounded and sandpapered, so there may be nothing to injure the fur. A mink fur stretcher makes an ideal fleshing board for muskrats, because it is just about the size and shape required.

Place the skin on the board fur side in, and with a dull knife proceed to remove all loose fat and flesh. An old table knife is a very handy tool for this purpose. When using a jackknife, care must be taken not to score or tear the pelt. The skin should be held taut with the left hand, while manipulating the knife with the right. Scrape by working from the head towards the base, or vice versa, being careful not to scrape the muscles behind the shoulders too close, because the ends of these are firmly attached to the skin. When all superfluous fat and flesh have been removed, the pelt is ready for the stretcher.

Fig. 3

There are various makes of steel and wire fur stretchers on the market, which can be purchased at a reasonable figure; but for the accommodation of muskrat pelts, I know of none better or cheaper than the common plain board stretchers which are made of dry goods boxes or similar material. These boards should be made of one-quarter-inch material, about thirty inches in length, six inches wide at the base and five and one-half inches wide at the shoulders. From the shoulders to the tip of the nose they should rapidly taper, coming to a point. This point should be rounded so as to fit the head snugly (See Fig. 3). The edges of the board should be nicely rounded and smoothly sandpapered. When boards are made of one-half-inch material, they should be beveled down to one-eighth of an inch at the edges. A quarter-inch hole should be drilled in each board near the base, so the pelts may be hung up when drying.

It will be remembered, as stated elsewhere in this work, that muskrats vary greatly in size in various parts of the country. This fact makes it impractical to quote exact dimensions for stretchers. The above dimensions are an approximate average for standard skins and are given to serve as an illustration for the guidance of the novice.

When stretching the fur, draw the pelts on to the stretcher, fur side in, in such a manner that the back squarely covers one side of the board (as illustrated), while the underside covers the other. Never stretch a pelt so carelessly that parts of both the back and underside appear on each side of the board. Draw the skin down firmly and fasten to the board by driving tacks all around the base. A tack should also be driven into the tip of nose and lower jaw to hold them in place.

The pelts should be hung up to cure in a cool, airy place; dampness causes mildew, which ruins them. Never dry furs in the sun or too near a fire, as this is liable to cause considerable damage. Never use salt or any other chemicals in curing pelts; allow them to dry by the natural process of evaporation. Be sure that they are held secure against mice and other pests.

Large quantities of the cheaper fur are made up and sold under fictitious names by the manufacturing furriers, such as "Hudson seal, river mink, coney, nutria," and others too numerous to mention. Hudson seal is the fur of muskrat, which is sheared, plucked, dyed and beautifully blended to imitate the fur seal. River mink is also the fur of muskrat prepared and dyed to a rich, deep brown to imitate the more valuable mink. Coney is a species of European rabbit, somewhat resembling our native cottontail, but the pelt of the former is firm and tough, which renders it fit for manufacturing purposes. Nutria is the commercial term for the fur of the South American coypou. These fancy names have been adopted, no doubt, so that the goods may sell better. For instance, that beautiful new "black sable" cloak, which is so soft and silky, and which Mrs. Brown is showing with so much pride to her neighbor Mrs. Smith, is in reality nothing more than the unadulterated fur of that despised animal, the skunk. Nevertheless, with the exception of the rare black fox, the skunk supplies the most beautiful and most durable natural black fur of North America. In the making up of this article, the white stripes in the fur are eliminated, as this is hair and not fur, as some people erroneously believe.

Select specimens of the cheaper fur, such as muskrat, opossum, etc., are prepared by skilled furriers to imitate the finer and more valuable furs; and when these craftsmen are through with their process of fixing, it would require the skill of an expert to distinguish the finished product from the genuine article which it imitates.

Though the manufacturing end of the business is of little interest to the trapper and small dealer in raw furs, I merely record the above statements to give the average reader an idea of how a large percentage of furs are skillfully camouflaged to improve their appearance and thus promote their sale.

In the following lines I shall endeavor to delineate, in an abridged form, the fundamentals and principles of "fur grading"; this, for the guidance of the reader, who, I shall presume, knows nothing about the art of grading and assorting raw furs. Be it remembered that in this, like in any other art or craft, the past master of that art or craft has from long experience acquired, unconsciously or otherwise, a certain "knack," the absence of which forms the main obstacle in the path of the novice. This fact again calls to mind the truth of that age old maxim, "Experience is the best teacher." What I am about to set forth here on the subject is done with the view in mind of assisting the amateur muskrat trapper (in whose interest this is written) to know and determine the value of his fur, which will enable him to realize more money on his catch and to find a better market for his goods. In my own days of adolescence as an amateur mink and muskrat trapper, it has been my privilege to handle and examine the pelts of hundreds of muskrats. This study and experience, alone, have been invaluable to me in buying and selling raw furs.

PELT: The inspection of the pelt or flesh side of a piece of fur is generally the first thing the fur buyer does, for the reason that the furs of most of the different animals are stretched and shipped to market pelt side out. The degree of primeness of any piece of fur is largely determined by the appearance of the pelt. To pass as No. 1, a pelt must possess a white, pink or flesh color. When blue spots are apparent on the pelts, they are termed blue-pelts or unprime. The value of these depends on the amount of blue showing on the pelts. When a pelt is possessed of but a few streaks or spots of blue, it is termed good unprime and goes into grade No. 2. The No. 3, or poor unprime, are those where the degree of primeness covers 40 per cent or more of the pelt. Any peltries below this plane of primeness are of little or no value.

With the exception of the muskrat and one or two others, the pelts of fur bearers are generally strictly prime during the latter part of November and the months of December, January and February, though occasionally an animal is caught during the latter part of November or early December whose pelt is not strictly prime, but these are exceptions. From this it can be readily seen that the appearance of blue-pelts in a trapper's collection of furs is due to early and late trapping. This trapping out of season should not be encouraged, and is now illegal in most states.

A pelt which has been damaged while killing or skinning its wearer, or in the process of fleshing, stretching and curing, cannot be classed as No. 1, though the pelt may be prime and the fur of good quality. Such pelts are classed as No. 2's, 3's, and trash, all depending on the amount of damage done. A pelt which has tainted or heated on account of flesh adhering, is considered valueless when the damage thus incurred loosens the fur and causes it to slip when handled; such peltries are termed trash and are unfit for any purpose. To avoid disaster, keep in mind the importance of properly fleshing the pelts as soon as they are taken off the animals.

FUR: Though the condition of the pelt is an important factor in determining the value of furs, the fur on fur side is of much more importance, also more difficult to grade and assort intelligently. The quality of the fur bespeaks the real value of the skin. The vital points for consideration are: density, length, color, sheen and superficial luster.

Blow into a piece of fur against the grain and you will notice two distinct layers. These are defined as inner or under fur, and top or guard hair. The former is the basis of the fur coat and on a No. 1 skin must exhibit a very dense growth. Pelts which possess a poor or thin coat of under fur are graded down. The guard hair forms the outer layer of the fur coat and must be sparse in density, but uniform throughout the pelt. The various shades of color and silky glossiness of these guard hairs harmonizing with the under fur is what gives the fur its natural beauty. Many a piece of fur will appear to be in first-class condition, but close scrutiny will often reveal the fact that guard hairs are missing in spots. This gives the fur a rugged or shaggy appearance. Furs possessing such defects cannot be made up in their natural state, but must be either sheared or plucked. On the grading sheet they are classified as "rubbed" and are graded down accordingly. This loss of guard hair is due to various reasons, principally the presence of parasites in the fur, which causes the animal to rub against foreign objects.

White fur, such as that of the ermine or Arctic fox, is valued as to the purity of its color. The pure or snow white pelts are the most valuable. Other shades in this class are gray white, blue white and yellowish to cream color. To command the highest market prices, it is essential that white fur be free from all blood stains.

The policy of color is reversed in the assorting of the black, brown, red and gray furs. Here the rule is, the darker the shades of the various colors, the more valuable the fur.

The mere color and beauty of certain furs of the same species often create a tremendous difference in the range of values. Let us, for example, consider the pelts of two foxes: We will say they are both large skins and perfectly prime, but one is a red, while the other is a black fox. Though both of these foxes may be of the same consanguinity, the pelt of the black would be worth about as many hundreds as that of the red would be worth dollars. In the case of the mink, otter, marten and other fine furs, a well furred pelt of dark color is often worth two or three times as much as a pale colored pelt of equal size and quality.

Towards spring many furs fade or grow pale in color, some are rubbed and the fur appears woolly. These are graded down and termed singed or "springy," and as a consequence are less valuable. To receive full value for raw furs, the tails must also receive proper attention. Where they are partly or wholly missing or have been damaged beyond redemption, the furs are discounted. This amounts to from ten to twenty-five per cent of the value of the pelt. All tails should be split a portion of their length and the bone removed, otherwise they are apt to spoil. The tails of muskrat, opossum and beaver are left on the carcass, as they have no fur value.

SIZE: There are three sizes of pelts, namely, large, medium and small; but dealers in raw furs find it necessary to quote a special grade for the very small or undersize skins. These kitts, as they are termed, are the skins of the young of late litters. They are not mature in pelt and the fur is of poor quality, hence of little value. A No. 1 large pelt is usually worth about twice as much as one of the same quality in the small size. From this the reader may gather that the large grade pelt must be twice the size of the small, but this is erroneous. The fact is, that in most species of fur bearers the variation in the large, medium and small size is but a difference of two or three inches in the length of the pelt. Just why there is such a radical difference in price is a mysterious prank of the fur trade, for which no one person is responsible. On the other hand, a small size pelt which is of good color and possesses a lustrous and dense coat of fur, is often worth as much or more than a large pelt of poor color. Remember that dimensions of the skin and primeness of pelt are of little consideration when the fur lacks quality.

GRADING MUSKRATS: Muskrats, unlike most other furs, are not strictly prime in pelt until early spring. For that reason they are assorted under three headings, as follows: Fall, winter and spring. The pelt of the fall muskrat displays very little primeness, but is endowed with a fairly dense growth of fur, and therefore is in good demand. The degree of primeness increases as the season advances, and when fifty per cent or more of the pelt is prime they are quoted as "Winter." When they are fully prime, which occurs during the latter part of February or early March, they are termed "Spring 'rats" and command the best prices.

Abnormally thin pelts are not uncommon among fur bearers, but this defect is most frequently found on muskrats. Just what causes this imperfection is not definitely known. The writer while trapping in the prairie region of Dakota caught both river and marsh 'rats, and discovered that the pelts of the latter were very thin, and when dry rattled like paper when handled; the color of the fur was a pale, rusty red and very dull compared with that of the pelts of the river 'rats in the same district. I believe the inferior quality of the fur of these marsh 'rats is due to the excessive amount of alkali present in the marshy waters of the Northwest. Papery peltries are discounted from ten to twenty-five per cent, because the leather of such thin pelted fur is delicate and not very lasting.

There is a larger percentage of kitts found in the average collection of fall muskrat pelts than among any other kind of fur. These pelts are poorly furred and very small compared with those of mature animals, and are of little value.

In the spring muskrats fight a great deal, especially the males. As a result, the pelts of these are often damaged considerably. It is not an uncommon occurrence to find entrapped muskrats so badly chewed and torn, by their own kind, that it does not pay to skin them.

In assorting muskrats, buyers usually pay more attention to size and primeness of pelt than they do to the fur, because it is generally conceded that the average run of 'rat fur is good. Nature endows the muskrat with a dense coat of fur, which, in fact, is a necessity to further its welfare in the icy waters in which it lives.

As before stated, 'rats, like most of the other fur bearers, vary considerably in size in various parts of the country. For example the pelt of a large Southwestern muskrat is no larger than that of an Atlantic coast 'rat of the small grade. The districts which show a marked difference in the value and size of 'rat pelts may be divided into four groups, as follows: First, Eastern Canada, New England, New York, Pennsylvania, New Jersey, Michigan, Ohio, Indiana, Illinois, and West Virginia; second, Delaware, Kentucky, Maryland,

Virginia, Tennessee, and the Carolinas; third, Wisconsin, Minnesota, Iowa, Nebraska, and the Northwest; fourth, Missouri, Arkansas, Kansas, to the Pacific and Southern.

The pelts of the first district are of the best quality and therefore command the best prices. Those of the second average about ten percent less per pelt, and those of the third and last district average about twenty and thirty-five percent less, respectively, than those of the first named district.

NOTE FROM THE EDITOR

I came across this manuscript by mistake. While searching for the work of the German post-war experimental writer, Arno Schmidt, I found what I thought was a book of his I hadn't previously encountered: *The Accomplished Muskrat Trapper*. Reading through the manuscript, it became apparent this was not the German writer's radical attempt at clarity, but an American Midwesterner sharing his expertise and love of muskrat trapping. Despite this realization, I continued to read. I instantly shared *The Accomplished Muskrat Trapper* with Kyle François and my brother Keegan Bohnsack, both people who I knew would appreciate my findings.

We know very little about *this* Arno Schmidt. There is no biography, no photos, no other surviving titles, if he published any more. Even his publisher is a mystery. When searching for Boyle Brothers publishing, results yield a seed processing company, a trucking service, a funeral home, among others. The West Loop address of the Chicago-based publisher is now a combination FedEx store and Jimmy John's sandwich shop, ironic in this instance for the franchise founder's past of hunting endangered

African animals. Everything that exists outside the text is a mystery to us.

So why publish this relatively unknown 100-year-old book? There are plenty of books on hunting, yet few that present the skill of trapping with such reverence for their catch. Schmidt observed muskrats. He notes their diet, their gestation period, and social behavior, all self-observed. He explains the most humane ways to trap and vouches for the safety of the trapper. He observes the industry and demands sustainability of his beloved "rats."

Following a trail does not always result in a catch, to use an obvious metaphor, but this was something we knew we had to pursue. The muskrat is not considered overtly remarkable, but in Schmidt's guide, he demonstrates beauty lies in the detail. I hope this persistence is as valuable to you as it has been for me.

Joshua Bohnsack

Arno E. Schmidt was a trapper and writer.

Kyle François is a writer, musician, and educator in Chicago. He was raised in rural Iowa where he learned to read, write, hunt, trap, garden, and sing. He was published in the first ever Long Day publication.

New & Forthcoming Titles

An Atavic Fear of Hailstorms
João Reis
Novella
ISBN: 9781950987290 • $14

Girl Thing
Morghen Tidd
Stories
ISBN: 9781950987368 • $14

Sex With My Family
Jessica Anne
Fictions
ISBN: 9781950987306 • $14

We Go Liquid
Christian TeBordo
Novel
ISBN: 9781950987412 • $16

LongDayPress.com   @LongDayPress